T0208158

My Testimony

A Journey To My New Beginning

VERONICA MARZETTE JOHNSON

authorHOUSE®

AuthorHouse™ LLC
1663 Liberty Drive
Bloomington, IN 47403
www.authorhouse.com
Phone: 1-800-839-8640

Published by AuthorHouse 04/18/2014

ISBN: 978-1-4969-0697-7 (sc)
ISBN: 978-1-4969-0696-0 (e)

Library of Congress Control Number: 2014907263

Any people depicted in stock imagery provided by Thinkstock are models, and such images are being used for illustrative purposes only. Certain stock imagery © *Thinkstock.*

This book is printed on acid-free paper.

Because of the dynamic nature of the Internet, any web addresses or links contained in this book may have changed since publication and may no longer be valid. The views expressed in this work are solely those of the author and do not necessarily reflect the views of the publisher, and the publisher hereby disclaims any responsibility for them.

This book is dedicated to my girls, Antoinette and Mia.

Stand firm on God's Word always.

I love you,

Mama

Contents

Acknowledgments

I thank God for everything. I could do nothing without Him.

To Gloria CJ, thank you for listening and advising. Thank you for planting the seed by the spirit for this book!

To my spiritual sisters, Evangelist Ethel Buchanan, Pastor Glyniel Garner, Pastor Tonja Williams and Lady Kimberly Smith, I love you so much and thank God for bringing us together!

To my pastor and first lady, Broderick and Venandee Hennington, of Integrity Bible Church, thank you for being such excellent spiritual parents. I love you!

To SJJ, thank you for sixteen years!

The Reason for the Story

And whatever you do in word or deed, do all in the name of the
Lord Jesus, giving thanks to God the Father through Him.
—Colossians 3:17 NKJV

The seed for writing this book was planted by the Lord through my friend Gloria. She and I have known each other for a little over ten years. We know each other's struggles, and we have been each other's encourager. She asked me on the afternoon of Wednesday, September 20, 2012, whether I had considered writing a book. From there, I could feel that my spirit bore witness to that suggestion. I always felt that the things I was going through were not in vain and that God would allow me to use them to help other people. There were times when I just wanted the onslaught to be over. I never thought of writing a book until God had her mention it to me. I have received confirmation several times from three different people regarding writing this book, and they didn't even realize it.

Just prior to the struggles I mention in this book, I attended a church service sometime around January or February of 2009 where the minister prophesized to me that I needed to buy a notebook and keep it by my bedside because God was about to begin telling me many things. The minister also told me that God was filling me with His Spirit to help me endure what was to come. I didn't understand what the minister was talking about at the time, but in hindsight, I understand exactly what he meant.

In the chapters of this book, I share the many things I learned while walking through my struggles. My pastor, Broderick D. Hennington of Integrity Bible Church in Birmingham, Alabama, said during one of his messages recently that a person has two testimonies: the one he or she tells to others and the one that's just between him or her and Jesus. This testimony is a little bit in between. I will be candid about a lot; however, some things I will keep between me and Jesus.

Some may wonder what makes my struggles so different from anyone else's. Some may even say that there are people who have gone through worse. To that I say, you are absolutely correct; there are people who have gone through worse things than I have. I also say my struggles were difficult and unique for me just like others' struggles are difficult and unique for them. I wrote this book to tell all who read it that they can make it through their difficulties with God's help. I also wrote this book to encourage people not to give up. I wrote it to inform people that struggles are temporary situations and warn them not to make permanent decisions based on their temporary situations.

This is a book about my journey to my new beginning. I will explain the things I learned from God while on this journey. I will tell all about God's goodness, grace, and love. I will tell all about what God did for me and how He came through for me many, many times. I will also tell of the many times God spoke to me through His Word, other people, dreams, and angelic visitations.

I admit the ride was bumpy—extremely bumpy. My friend Gloria once gave me a card that was humorous but so very true. It read, "This too shall pass. Painful, like a kidney stone; but it will pass." The inside of the card told me to hang on in there. It was so funny, but it helped me put things in perspective and keep my focus on God. Yes, we go through struggles. Yes, those struggles hurt. But they pass and we are made better people if we allow God to put us back together again.

I hope you are encouraged by *My Testimony—A Journey to My New Beginning*!

Introduction: The Beginning of It All

Those who sow in tears; shall reap in joy. He who continually
goes forth weeping, Bearing seed for sowing. Shall doubtless
come again with rejoicing, bringing his sheaves with him.
—Psalm 126:5–6 NKJV

This is the story that God has allowed me to tell of the struggles I faced and overcame with His help. Some of these struggles were caused by outside influences, and some were brought about by my own bad decision making. The most recent years were difficult for me. My difficulties may not have been as bad as another person's, but they were my struggles nonetheless.

I am telling my story to encourage others not to give up. God is on your side. Some may ask what makes my struggles so much different from another person's. Some people are battling cancer. Some are in the throes of domestic violence. My struggles were and still are emotional. I have emotional battle scars. I am healing from a broken heart—or, shall I say, a shattered heart. I always say that emotional scars are lingering scars. One may seem fine on the outside, while on the inside, there may be a battle raging. I know for me there was a constant war. I felt pain continuously. There was a gnawing ache in my heart all the time. I did my best to plant seeds of encouragement in others because I wanted that harvest for myself. I didn't want to be in pain, but I knew self-destructive behavior, such as drinking, smoking, and partying, wouldn't make it better. I prayed a lot. I cried a lot. I was quiet all the time.

In four short years (2009–2013), I lost my father, my mother, my marriage, and my home. The enemy attacked my reputation and even tried to come against my daughters. I suffered through financial difficulties. I was unable to pay my bills. There were times when I thought my power, gas, or water would be turned off. My credit went down the drain. I had to deal with helping my daughters maintain their emotional stability. My youngest daughter almost had to repeat a grade because she was struggling with some issues. But *God*! As the song states, if it had not been for the Lord on my side, tell me, where would I be?

Many did not understand how I was feeling. I had a particularly hard time at work. I guess people think if you aren't dealing with a physical ailment, then you can just "get over" things (as I was once told by one of my former bosses). I had difficulties concentrating. I had trouble remembering things. There was so much on my mind. Many times, my supervisors would get impatient with me because they thought I wasn't being effective in my job. In reality, I had too much on my plate. As a result, my confidence was being chipped away little by little. I began to second-guess my ability, and I ultimately stopped trying.

I talked to an employee assistance program (EAP) counselor at work once regarding issues I was encountering there. I told her about the stresses at home and how I was being treated at work. Honestly, I was not being treated well at work. I was being disrespected daily. The EAP counselor told me that I was having problems because I never had the opportunity to properly grieve all of the losses I had incurred. She said as soon as the first crisis ended, another one was right behind it. The counselor further said there was nothing wrong with me; I just had too many things to deal with at one time. Hearing that restored some of my confidence.

Prior to 2009, my family withstood some challenges that hurt tremendously. From 2005 until June 17, 2012, I took care of my mother, who had been diagnosed with a mental illness called schizoaffective disorder. In layman's terms, this is a combination of bipolar disorder and paranoid schizophrenia. However, I believe the struggle in my family actually began January 8, 1992. This was the day that my brother, my only sibling, was killed. He was twenty-six years old, unmarried, and had no children. Up until that moment, my family life was pretty uneventful. My parents, brother, and I lived in the Bronx, New York. My father was a detective with the New York City Police Department. My mother was a nursing supervisor. My brother and I went to school, hung out with our friends, and did normal teenage things. The four of us were really close. We took a lot of family trips. We weren't rich, but all of our needs and a lot of our wants were met. Nothing dramatic ever happened—until the day my brother died.

I had been working at the US Postal Service for almost a year when my dad came to my job to tell me about my brother's death. I had never felt so much pain in my life. It felt like someone had punched me in the stomach and kept punching. My chest hurt. My head hurt. Everything hurt. I believed in God, but I had never had a deep relationship with Him. I never knew that the Word said that we must worship God in spirit and in truth. All I knew was how badly this whole thing hurt. Watching my parents grieve was difficult. I always viewed them as the strongest two people in the world, and now I was watching them (yes, my dad too) cry. This was when I started looking at God a little differently. Before, I prayed and went to church, but it was more of a ritual. Now, I was looking for answers. I wasn't angry at God; I just wanted to know why. I was really angry at my brother for getting himself killed. I was angry with him for putting himself in harm's way and leaving me. Now who would my best friend be?

I remember several days after my brother's funeral, my father was talking about how our family had been affected. He equated our situation to the story of Job. In the book of Job, the title character lived a fruitful, rich life. He had many children, land, money, and so on. Everything looked great for Job. He was prosperous. Then, calamity struck just like it struck our family. I remember my father wondering why this all happened to us, just as Job had done. I remember my father questioning God, just like Job had done. I even remember my father wondering if this was part of our destiny.

Now that I know and understand the book of Job, I can see several similarities in that particular period of my life and the Bible story. Just as Job feared something bad would happen to his children, we often worried that something bad would happen to my brother. He hung around the wrong people, even though he was a good-hearted person. He had a drug problem. That fear opened the door to the enemy and allowed him to come in and do damage to our family. However, I didn't spend a lot of time questioning God because I didn't want to face the same round of questions God asked Job.

Fast-forward to around the year 2000. My mother announced that she was divorcing my father after thirty-seven years of marriage. Even though I was almost forty years old at the time and had my own family, this hit me really hard. I felt like my home base had fallen apart. I also felt that my parents were not following the advice they had given me and my husband. My father told us both that we didn't divorce in our family. The way in which my mother left angered me. She moved out of their home taking all of the furniture while my father was on a business trip. When he arrived home, he was shocked to see everything was gone. My mother was angry with me because I would not come help her move that day. I felt it was not the right thing to do to my own father. My mother felt I was taking sides, but I would not have done that to her either. She never quite seemed to understand that part.

Fast-forward again to around the year 2005, my mother began showing very pronounced symptoms of mental illness. I initially thought she had early onset dementia. She began accusing me of taking things from her and began forgetting things. One day, she told me about hallucinations she saw in her house. I also found notes around her house with odd requests written on them. As the years progressed, she got worse. She began making frequent visits to the hospital. During one hospital stay, I specifically asked if my mother had dementia. The doctor told me she did not and gave me her diagnosis. My family was always in an upheaval because we never knew when something was going to happen.

On January 8, 1992, my brother, my only sibling, was killed. In 2001, my parents' divorced. On April 6, 2009, the unthinkable happened—my father died suddenly. On June 17, 2010, it happened again—my mother died. On my birthday, December 26, 2010, the unthinkable happened once again—my husband left (the first time). Three consecutive blows—boom, boom, boom!

In May 2011, *boom*, there was another emotional blow—my divorce was final.

In May 2013, *boom* again—I had to move from my house and rent a town house.

In November 2013, *boom*—it was the closing on the short sale of my house.

In January 2014, boom, early retirement. While this is considered a good thing, my retirement was emotional for me. It felt like a loss as well as a gain. I was losing life as I knew it, but I was gaining a brand-new life and opportunity to do some things careerwise that I wanted to do.

In the aftermath of these emotional strikes, I learned many, many things about myself and mostly about God. These things helped me immediately after I received each blow. I am still learning even now.

Being Born Again Will Help You Deal with Life's Problems

There was a man of the Pharisees named Nicodemus, a ruler
of the Jews. This man came to Jesus by night and said to Him,
"Rabbi, we know that you are a teacher come from God; for
no one can do these signs that you do unless God is with him."
Jesus answered and said to him, "Most assuredly, I say to you,
unless one is born again, he cannot see the kingdom of God."
—John 3:1–3 NKJV

I took my parents' divorce very hard. I felt like my home base was
falling apart. I began seeing a counselor through the employee
assistance program at work. The counselor suggested that I take
antidepressants—Celera, I think it was. I took it for about two weeks
until I talked to one of my aunts on the phone. I told her about the
counselor I was seeing and that I was taking antidepressants. She told me,
"You don't need antidepressants. You need Jesus. You need to give Him
any problem you have. Now, flush those pills down the toilet." That was
exactly what I did. I flushed those pills down the toilet, and when I went
to Bible study at church during the week, I gave my life to Jesus. I am
not recommending that everyone stop taking prescription medicines.
Go to your doctor before stopping any prescription medication. This is
what I did, and for me, it worked out for the best.

1

I believe the many things I learned during this period will be beneficial to you, but what is most needful above anything is a relationship with Jesus Christ. John 3:16 says, "For God so loved that world that he gave his only begotten son that whosoever believeth in him shall not perish but have everlasting life." Mankind was lost because of the sin that entered the world with the disobedience of Adam and Eve. But God loved mankind too much to allow sin to separate Him from us. Since God requires a blood sacrifice to atone for sin, God came to earth in the form of Jesus Christ to be that blood sacrifice so we would not have to answer for sin. A relationship with Jesus Christ does not mean an end to all problems, but you will be guaranteed victory in all "battles" because you do have a relationship with Jesus Christ.

Romans 1:16–17 says, "For I am not ashamed of the gospel of Christ, for it is the power of God to salvation for everyone who believes, for the Jew first and also for the Greek. For in it the righteousness of God is revealed from faith to faith; as it is written, 'The just shall live by faith.'"

I had to put my pride aside and not worry about what other people thought about me. I also had to come to grips with the fact that though I had been in church all my life, I really was not saved. I had to make that decision for myself. I am here today to say I am not ashamed of the gospel of Jesus Christ.

Romans 2:4 says, "Or do you despise the riches of His goodness, forbearance, and longsuffering, not knowing that the goodness of God leads you to repentance?"

I was under the deception that since I was in the church and my life had gone fairly well that I was going to heaven. I didn't realize that God's goodness toward me had nothing to do with me. God was good to me because He wanted me to turn from my life of sin to Him.

Romans 3:23–25 says,

> For all have sinned and fall short of the glory of God, being justified freely by His grace through the redemption that is in Christ Jesus, whom God set forth as a propitiation by His blood, through faith, to demonstrate His righteousness, because in His forbearance God had passed over the sins that were previously committed.

Romans 5:8–11 says,

> But God demonstrates His own love toward us, in that while we were still sinners, Christ died for us. Much more then, having now been justified by His blood, we shall be saved from wrath through Him. For if when we were enemies we were reconciled to God through the death of His Son, much more, having been reconciled, we shall be saved by His life. And not only that, but we also rejoice in God through our Lord Jesus Christ, through whom we have now received the reconciliation.

Romans 6:23 says, "For the wages of sin is death, but the gift of God is eternal life in Christ Jesus our Lord."

Though I have lived a life of sin, God declares me righteous because of the shed blood of Jesus. Through this act, I have been reconciled (back in relationship) to God. If I did not accept this free gift from God, I would have to accept the punishment for my own sins by going to hell. He didn't do this just for me but for all of us.

Romans 10:9–13 says,

> If you confess with your mouth the Lord Jesus and believe in your heart that God has raised Him from the dead, you will be saved. For with the heart one believes unto righteousness, and with the mouth confession is made unto salvation. For the Scripture says, "Whoever believes on Him will not be put to shame. For there is no distinction between Jew and Greek, for the same Lord over all is rich to all who call upon Him. For "whoever calls on the name of the Lord shall be saved."

I believe that Jesus was crucified, died, and rose from the dead, and I made Him the Lord of my life. And you can do the same.

A relationship with Jesus Christ made it easier for me to deal with life difficulties. Again, it's no guarantee that bad things will never happen, but it's an assurance that you have God Himself on your side to help you through difficulties. Plus, *Jesus is the only way to God!*

God loves you, and He wants to be in a relationship with you. Your past has nothing to do with God's love for you. He's not condemning you. If you want to accept Jesus Christ as your Lord and Savior; say the prayer below.

Prayer for Salvation

Dear Heavenly Father, I admit I am a sinner and I repent of every sin I have committed. I believe that Jesus Christ is the Son of God. I believe that He was crucified, died, was buried and rose from the dead. I thank you, Lord, for your love for me. I make Jesus the Lord of my life on this day and receive salvation. In Jesus's name, amen.

If you said this prayer or one similar, you are now saved. You are a child of God. Congratulations! Meditate on Romans 8:16–17, "The Spirit Himself bears witness with our spirit that we are children of God, and if children, then heirs—heirs of God and joint heirs with Christ, if indeed we suffer with Him, that we may also be glorified together."

In retrospect, I now know that I needed to put God first. Matthew 6:33 says, "Seek ye first the kingdom of God and His righteousness and all other things will be added unto thee." I went to church while growing up. I participated in all the church programs and did all of the church stuff. My grandfather was a pastor. I thought I had the inside track on church stuff. But I had things backward. I did not know that I was to put God first. I did not know that I was to look to Him only. I would pray and ask God to bless things without ever asking Him if it was something He even wanted me to do. I figured if it was a good thing, it was okay to do it. I never bothered to find out whether it was a "God thing."

I learned that I needed to be in a relationship with God. I needed to connect to God spiritually. In John 4:24, it says, "God is spirit, and his worshipers must worship in the Spirit and in truth." I always thought that as long as I was in church and did good things, I was okay. My worship was from the outside in, not from the inside out. I did not know that I could be in a relationship with God. I always thought I had to remain distant from God because He was big and mighty. I never knew how much He loved me and wanted to be in a relationship with me.

I learned what it says in Ephesians 6:12, "For our struggle is not against flesh and blood, but against the rulers, against the authorities, against the powers of this dark world and against the spiritual forces of evil in the heavenly realms." I did not know that some of my battles were orchestrated by God's and mankind's enemy, Satan! I did not know about *my* authority against the enemy.

Finally, I learned that God had a plan for my life. In Jeremiah 29:11, God speaks to Jeremiah about Israel's captivity when he says, "'For I know the plans I have for you,' declares the LORD, 'plans to prosper you and not to harm you, plans to give you hope and a future.'" Just as Israel thought their fate was dismal, God was encouraging them. Just as my family thought our fate was dismal because of my brother's death, I began to find out over time that God had a plan for me and the plan was a good one. I began to find out that this plan didn't begin with my brother's death but was created before I was even conceived.

LESSON #2

There Is No Condemnation

There is therefore now no condemnation to them which are in Christ Jesus, who walk not after the flesh, but after the Spirit.
—Romans 8:1 NKJV

When my husband left me, I was devastated even though I put up a brave front. He left three times. The first time was on my birthday, which was six months after my mother died. He returned for about a day and left again. He stayed for almost two weeks and left a third time. That time was it. I couldn't let his constant coming in and going out disrupt our children. I now see why God says He hates divorce. It is devastating to everyone involved. It is devastating to both spouses and to the children. It confuses friends and extended family members. My parents' divorce was devastating enough, now I was going through the same thing.

The part that really hurt was I was accused of doing something that I did not do. The accusation was so far from my character, yet to my husband, it was true. It was bad enough I was losing my husband and my family, but it was for something that I didn't do. How do you apologize for that? My husband's leaving hurt and him telling me that he no longer loved me hurt even more. It crushed my heart. I kept thinking, *I can't believe this is happening. I took sacred vows with this man. How can he drop me like that and tell me he doesn't love me?* My marriage needed some work, but I was not planning to leave.

In the midst of everything, Satan was in my ear talking, condemning me of past and present mistakes. He was just doing what John 10:10 says he does: "The thief cometh not, but for to steal, and to kill, and to destroy: I am come that they might have life, and that they might have it more abundantly." The Lord even told me one morning that Satan wished to sift me as wheat. I knew I wasn't perfect. I had made my share of mistakes. But I didn't think they were bad enough to lose my entire marriage. For fourteen years, I did the best I could. I tried to take care of the house, the kids, my husband, work, see about my parents, etc., but were my mistakes enough to lose everything I held dear?

I did make a mistake that Satan tried to use to bring me down. I found a lot of family members and friends on Facebook. One particular friend I found after not hearing from him for fifteen years. His profile stated he was saved just like me. He had pictures of his wife, children, and grandchildren. So, when I sent him a friend request, I thought nothing of it. For months, we sent occasional messages through Facebook. Then, we exchanged phone numbers and gradually started texting and talking on the phone. Occasionally turned into daily. Then, one day, we met for lunch. *Fatal mistake!* The emotional affair really began then. We started relying on each other for advice. We told each other intimate details of our marriages, things that were reserved for our spouses only. I felt justified because my husband seemed distant from me at the time. I was lonely, and my friend was lonely too. I got the compliments and the attention that I wanted, and so did he. He had lunch with me, something my husband always said he didn't have time for.

When things fell apart in my marriage, I felt extremely guilty. The enemy told me:

"You're a failure!"

"No one wants you!"

"You messed up real bad!"

"Now your kids will hate you because you
busted up their happy home!"

"Your husband left you because you were a lousy wife!"

"You're ugly. No one will want you!"

"You're fat. No man wants a fat woman!"

"You're stupid!"

"You're a whore!"

"Your husband doesn't want you."

"Your family doesn't want you."

"You have no friends."

"You're unlikeable!"

The Bible story about the woman caught in adultery, told in John 8:1–12
reads:

> Jesus went unto the Mount of Olives. And early in the
> morning he came again into the temple, and all the
> people came unto him; and he sat down, and taught
> them. And the scribes and Pharisees brought unto him
> a woman taken in adultery; and when they had set her
> in the midst, they said unto him, Master, this woman
> was taken in adultery, in the very act. Now Moses in

the law commanded us, that such should be stoned: but what sayest thou?

This they said, tempting him that they might have to accuse him. But Jesus stooped down, and with his finger wrote on the ground, as though he heard them not. So when they continued asking him, he lifted up himself, and said unto them, He that is without sin among you, let him first cast a stone at her. And again he stooped down, and wrote on the ground. And they which heard it, being convicted by their own conscience, went out one by one, beginning at the eldest, even unto the last: and Jesus was left alone, and the woman standing in the midst.

When Jesus had lifted up himself, and saw none but the woman, he said unto her, Woman, where are those thine accusers? Hath no man condemned thee?

She said, No man, Lord.

And Jesus said unto her, Neither do I condemn thee: go, and sin no more.

Then spake Jesus again unto them, saying, I am the light of the world: he that followeth me shall not walk in darkness, but shall have the light of life.

The Bible story about the woman at the well, John 4:1–29 reads:

When therefore the Lord knew how the Pharisees had heard that Jesus made and baptized more disciples than John, (Though Jesus himself baptized not, but his disciples,) He left Judaea, and departed again into

Galilee. And he must needs go through Samaria. Then cometh he to a city of Samaria, which is called Sychar, near to the parcel of ground that Jacob gave to his son Joseph. Now Jacob's well was there. Jesus therefore, being wearied with his journey, sat thus on the well: and it was about the sixth hour. There cometh a woman of Samaria to draw water: Jesus saith unto her, Give me to drink. (For his disciples were gone away unto the city to buy meat.)

Then saith the woman of Samaria unto him, How is it that thou, being a Jew, askest drink of me, which am a woman of Samaria? for the Jews have no dealings with the Samaritans.

Jesus answered and said unto her, If thou knewest the gift of God, and who it is that saith to thee, Give me to drink; thou wouldest have asked of him, and he would have given thee living water.

The woman saith unto him, Sir, thou hast nothing to draw with, and the well is deep: from whence then hast thou that living water? Art thou greater than our father Jacob, which gave us the well, and drank thereof himself, and his children, and his cattle?

Jesus answered and said unto her, Whosoever drinketh of this water shall thirst again: But whosoever drinketh of the water that I shall give him shall never thirst; but the water that I shall give him shall be in him a well of water springing up into everlasting life.

The woman saith unto him, Sir, give me this water, that I thirst not, neither come hither to draw.

Jesus saith unto her, Go, call thy husband, and come hither.

The woman answered and said, I have no husband.

Jesus said unto her, Thou hast well said, I have no husband: For thou hast had five husbands; and he whom thou now hast is not thy husband: in that saidst thou truly.

The woman saith unto him, Sir, I perceive that thou art a prophet. Our fathers worshipped in this mountain; and ye say, that in Jerusalem is the place where men ought to worship.

Jesus saith unto her, Woman, believe me, the hour cometh, when ye shall neither in this mountain, nor yet at Jerusalem, worship the Father. Ye worship ye know not what: we know what we worship: for salvation is of the Jews. But the hour cometh, and now is, when the true worshippers shall worship the Father in spirit and in truth: for the Father seeketh such to worship him. God is a Spirit: and they that worship him must worship him in spirit and in truth.

The woman saith unto him, I know that Messias cometh, which is called Christ: when he is come, he will tell us all things.

Jesus saith unto her, I that speak unto thee am he.

And upon this came his disciples, and marvelled that he talked with the woman: yet no man said, What seekest thou? or, Why talkest thou with her?

> The woman then left her waterpot, and went her way into the city, and saith to the men, Come, see a man, which told me all things that ever I did: is not this the Christ?

Both women made mistakes, just like I did. People probably talked about both women, just like they may have about me. However, Jesus *still* spoke to them, just like He spoke to me. Jesus *did not* reject them, and He hasn't rejected me. Jesus *did not* condemn them, and He did not condemn me. Jesus showed both women mercy, love, and forgiveness, and He showed me the same things. If Jesus did this for these two women and for me, what's to stop Him from doing it for you? Just like I had to make a decision, you have to make a decision as well. Are you going to allow the enemy to continue to speak condemnation to you, or will you open your mouth and speak. I decided to speak, and I advise you to do the same!

Just as Jesus did while He was being tempted in the wilderness, I also began telling Satan, "It is written..." After I repented of my part in the divorce and in the emotional affair, I was cleansed of all unrighteousness, as the Word says (1 John 8:9: "If we confess our sins, he is faithful and just to forgive us our sins, and to cleanse us from all unrighteousness.")

When Satan came to remind me of my mistakes (real and exaggerated), I began to remind him of who God says I am. I bought a prayer book that I use often called *Prayers That Rout Demons* by John Eckhart. In his book, Mr. Eckhart includes various prayer and daily confessions that I use, such as:

> "I am established in righteousness, and oppression is far from me" (Isaiah 54:14).

> "I do not have the spirit of fear but power, love and a sound mind" (2 Timothy 1:7).

"I am called in Christ" (Romans 1:6).

"I am a joint heir with Christ" (Romans 8:17).

"I have been chosen in Christ before the foundation of the world that I should be holy and without blame before him" (Ephesians 1:4).

"I have been created in Christ unto good works" (Ephesians 2:10).

"Christ in me is the hope of glory" (Colossians 1:27).

"I am complete in Christ" (Colossians 2:10).

"I have the mind of Christ" (1 Corinthians 2:16).

I also received wise, godly counsel from my pastor and from my spiritual sisters and friends. They reminded me of what God says about me and how I am no longer under any condemnation. They helped rebuild my confidence and give me the strength to keep pushing even though there were times when I just wanted to give up.

As I said before, I felt extremely guilty about getting a divorce. During a counseling session, my pastor had me read 1 Corinthians 7:12–15:

> But to the rest speak I, not the Lord: If any brother hath a wife that believeth not, and she be pleased to dwell with him, let him not put her away. And the woman which hath an husband that believeth not, and if he be pleased to dwell with her, let her not leave him. For the unbelieving husband is sanctified by the wife, and the unbelieving wife is sanctified by the husband: else were your children unclean; but now are they holy. But if

the unbelieving depart, let him depart. A brother or a sister is not under bondage in such cases: but God hath called us to peace.

Prior to going into the counseling session with my pastor, one of my friends texted me the same scripture. When my pastor discussed the scripture, I could feel a heaviness lift off of me. It was as though God was letting me know that He was not mad at me and He was not condemning me. It was confirmation for me that I had a biblical reason for getting a divorce. This is not to suggest that everyone seek out biblical reasons to divorce their spouses. I would suggest that couples whose marriages are in trouble do everything possible to remain together. But, for me, this scripture removed the condemnation that Satan was trying to place on me.

We all make mistakes. We all fall short. Sometimes, other people will forgive us. Sometimes they will not. What's important is that God forgives you, and you must forgive yourself. Do not allow yourself to walk in condemnation.

LESSON #3

Don't Receive Everything Others Say about You

But you are a chosen people, a royal priesthood, a holy nation,
God's special possession, that you may declare the praises of him
who called you out of darkness into his wonderful light. Once
you were not a people, but now you are the people of God; once
you had not received mercy, but now you have received mercy.
—1 Peter 2:9–10 NKJV

While I was taking care of my mom, she said many, many hurtful things to me. She told me that I was a thief. She said I was trying to hurt her. She said I was going to hell. She called me disrespectful and ungrateful. However, my mom said these things during her illness. She was diagnosed with schizoaffective disorder, which is a combination of bipolar disorder and schizophrenia. As her illness progressed, she said even more hurtful things that always seemed to be directed at me. She never said hurtful things to her sister or brother, her neighbors, anyone from church, or anyone else—always me. I realized those words were coming from her illness and were directed at me because I was her primary caregiver. But sometimes they cut like a knife. I really had to pray.

When my husband and I were going through a difficult time just before he left, he said things to me that were hurtful. He called me a "bald-faced liar" one day. During a trip to the emergency room for a stomach ailment, he insinuated that I poisoned him. He constantly accused me of plotting with someone to kill him. He called the police early one morning and told the officer I was plotting to kill him. He accused me of letting men in the house during the night while he was at work. One of the last things he told me really cut like a knife. He told me he no longer loved me. There were many other hurtful things that he said. I really did not understand where these accusations came from, and I do not understand them to this day. It hurt me and angered me because I was losing my marriage and family because of something that was not true. The actions I was accused of were totally out of character for me, and I felt he should know me better. I really had to pray.

On my job (while I was going through these things with my husband), I had one boss who told me I was the "worst secretary in the world." I had one who told me, "Don't bring your problems to work." I had another who told me to "hurry up and get things fixed." One boss yelled and screamed at me. This particular boss did nothing but look for the worst in me, and what is so ironic is that God told me to give this person a quiet and soft answer to everything. The more I did so, the more this boss yelled and screamed at me, frequently trying to publicly humiliate me by yelling and screaming at me. On one occasion, this boss even used a lower-level employee to show me how to do my job. I was told that that boss held the key to whether I got another job. This boss even attempted to set me up to fail, tried to ruin my reputation with other people at work, told me it was torture working with me and that *no one* liked me, and put me out of the office just before I retired.

The Bible says in Proverbs 18:21, "The tongue has the power of life and death, and those who love it will eat its fruit." I had some very hurtful things spoken to me by some of my bosses, those closest to me, and those for whom I was supposed to show respect. Even though I knew who I was in Christ, their words still pierced my very soul like a knife. I cried a lot, and I prayed a lot.

During these difficult times, God reminded me of who I was in Him. I mediated on "I am established in righteousness, and oppression is far from me" (Isaiah 54:14) and "But you are a chosen people, a royal priesthood, a holy nation, God's special possession, that you may declare the praises of him who called you out of darkness into his wonderful light" (1 Peter 2:9).

While I was praying one day about how I was being treated at work, God reminded me of the story of Balak and Balaam in Numbers 22 through 23. In this story, Balak became fearful of Israel because they had a reputation of defeating their foes and God made them numerous. Because Balak was fearful of Israel, he hired the prophet Balaam to put a curse on Israel. However, God would not allow Balaam to curse Israel: "But God said to Balaam, 'Do not go with them. You must not put a curse on those people, because they are blessed'" (Numbers 22:12). As I was being mistreated at work, God told me that I had nothing to fear because I was blessed and no one could curse me. One day in the middle of one of my bosses yelling at me, I heard God say, "Don't worry about them. They are a nonissue." It was very comforting for me, but at the same time, it was really funny to me. Here I am being yelled at, and God intervenes on my behalf. I think I may have had some kind of smirk on my face because my boss seemed to get even madder at me.

I was also reminded of how the Israelites were sent to spy out the land the Lord had given them in the book of Numbers. There were ten spies, including Joshua and Caleb. When the spies arrived in the land the Lord promised them, they saw that everything was big in the land, even the people. The people were descendants of Anak and were giants. When the spies returned and gave their report to Moses and Aaron, eight of the spies gave a negative report. They reported truthfully that there were giants, *but* they also said they were grasshoppers compared to the people in the land. Who told them they were grasshoppers? But Joshua and Caleb told Moses and Aaron that they were able to take the giants because God was on their side. They believed what God said. The Israelites did not go into the Promised Land because of the report of the eight spies. To make things worse, God said they would wander in the wilderness for forty years because of their unbelief. At the end of the forty years, after those particular people died, Joshua, Caleb, and the children of the spies were able to take the land.

Finally, I am reminded of my Lord and Savior Jesus Christ. When He was being tortured and crucified, the Bible says He did not say a word. In due time, He was raised from the dead for all to see.

God spoke the following things to me regarding the words people speak to me or about me:

1. Believe what God says.
2. I do not have to receive anything that does not line up with God's Word.
3. I can cancel any word curses the enemy tries to place on me by way of someone else's words.
4. Forgive those who speak ill of you.
5. Do not retaliate.
6. Encourage yourself in the Lord.
7. Keep doing well.

    a. Meditate on the Word. Renew your mind.
    b. "Do not conform to the pattern of this world, but be transformed by the renewing of your mind. Then you will be able to test and approve what God's will is—his good, pleasing and perfect will" (Romans 12:2).

8. Not all criticism is negative criticism. There may be some truth to what they are saying.

a. I heard Bishop T. D. Jakes say once to "chew the meat and spit out the bones." Extract those things that may be true, and make adjustments.

9. Don't call yourself a "grasshopper."

On October 11, 2012, God spoke the following things to me, and they were really an encouragement:

> Do not worry about what the enemy says. I am your shield. I am your hedge of protection. I am your covering. The enemy is angry because he can't move you. Keep on the armor. Put it all on. You've been leaving some pieces off, and that's why your feelings are getting hurt. Keep it on. Read Ephesians 6. Don't bow to the golden image. I am your God. I am your source. I am all you need. Look to me. When you are in the furnace, I will be there. Don't worry or fret. I contend with those who contend with you. You will not lose your job. I will turn their words back on them. My word says as long as the earth remains, there will be seed time and harvest. The enemy's [name purposely deleted] harvest is about to spring forth, and many of their crops are rotten. I will repay. I am the vindicator. Do not plot revenge. I love them, but they have not obeyed. You did well with the assignment, but you are getting weary. Keep your mouth shut. I am guarding your heart. No worries. Look to me. There is much for you to do. I am making you stronger. These are your resistant weighs to build your spiritual muscles. I put what's needed in you so you can do this. You will not die or go under. Don't worry about who does or doesn't love you. I love you. Take in My love. Not just in your mind but in your spirit. Worship Me in spirit and in

truth. I am yours, and you are Mine always. I am in love with you. I will treat you right for I am your God. I love you with an everlasting love. Those who do "the enemy's" bidding will be dealt with. No worry. I am in control. You don't see in the spirit realm. The angels are all around you ready to fight for you. Be ready. I am speaking on your behalf. There are those who are trying to bring you down, but they can't. I am your backbone. I hold you up and always will. I love you.

I learned that I am in charge of those things I allow to stay in my soul. I learned that God loves me beyond a shadow of a doubt. I learned that I have value. The Word says that I have authority to tread on snakes and scorpions and nothing by any means shall hurt me. No matter what someone says about me, it doesn't mean that I have to receive it. Self-esteem is just that; it belongs to "my-self." Even though the hurtful thing was said, it doesn't mean that I take it in as true.

I posted the following on my Facebook page to remind myself and others not to receive everything said: "Don't receive everything someone says about you, especially if it doesn't line up with God's Word. Trust God and believe *His* report! I am not a flunky or a failure. I am the righteousness of God; I am an heir with Christ; I am saved by grace; I am a daughter of the King. I can do all things through Christ Jesus!"

My spiritual big sister Prophetess-Evangelist Ethel Buchanan told me once, "Sometimes what's obvious is not what people see and remember the most. Buried treasure isn't seen until it's searched for. You have value!"

I will believe God's report about me and not the report of the enemy. I suggest you do the same.

LESSON #4

You Can't Go by What Things Look Like on the Outside; Trust God; Have Faith!

Then Caleb silenced the people before Moses and said we should go up and take possession of the land for we can certainly do it.
—Numbers 13:30 NKJV

Each struggle that I experienced seemed to become more intense. I thought my mom's illness was the worst thing. It was very difficult watching my mom change as her mind got further and further away from me. It was difficult because I wanted the "mommy" I had had as a child, teenager, and young woman. I wanted my kids to have their grandma back.

But I lived through it!

I thought dealing with my parents' divorce was the worst thing in the world. I just couldn't believe their marriage was over. They had been married so long, thirty-seven years to be exact. They were my example of how to stay together. Their marriage was even the envy of some people. Holidays, birthdays, and other special occasions were not easy as I watched them on opposite sides, seemingly making us have to choose between the two of them. The thing that hurt was when my father started dating immediately after he and my mom separated; then he finally ended up living with one of his girlfriends. He seemed like such a hypocrite because he always taught me not to "shack up" with anyone. I wanted my parents back together. I wanted that woman just to disappear. I wanted my family back the way it was.

But I lived through it!

I thought dealing with my parents' deaths was the worst thing in the world. To me, my parents were superheroes. They would live forever in my eyes. My brother was already gone, but I still had my parents. Then, when my father died, I thought, *I still have my mother.* Then my mom died. There I was standing alone—so I thought. I felt such emptiness and hurt.

But I lived through it!

With my brother and my parents gone, I thought, *At least I have my husband and my girls.* Little did I know that was about to change. My husband kept hinting that he was leaving. He kept asking me questions about my intentions of staying in the marriage. I couldn't understand why he was asking me questions like that. I had no intention of leaving him. Then, he stopped having his paycheck direct-deposited in a checking account we were both using and put into one that only he had access to. Finally, he left.

But I lived through it!

Soon after he left, the money problems began. I was thankful we did not have a lot of debt. We had no credit-card bills or car notes. The only bills we had were utility bills, the house note, and school expenses for the girls. But with the household income being cut tremendously, it got harder and harder to make ends meet. Initially, my husband said he wasn't going to give me anything, but he had a change of heart and started giving me support. I even had to make withdrawals from the retirement three times to help with bills. There were times when the cable was disconnected. The trash can was confiscated because of nonpayment. The telephone was disconnected. I was grateful none of the utilities were disconnected until recently. The gas was disconnected the day before it snowed. So we had no heat and no hot water. I also could not use the stove, so I couldn't cook. God moved on my ex-husband's heart, and he invited us to stay at his house until the gas bill was paid. He even gave me some extra money to help pay the bill.

I received notification from my mortgage company that they were going to foreclose on the house. I had tried for months to obtain a loan modification and got the runaround. I was approved on a trial basis and successfully made it through that. Then, I was approved for the modification. *Finally, some stability,* I thought. I completed the paperwork and returned it with a certified check. I then received a letter stating I hadn't completed a form correctly. When I called to inquire about the form, I could not get a straight answer. About two weeks later, I received another letter disapproving the modification.

I then begin working with a law firm in Utah that was supposed to help me get a loan modification, and I got the runaround from them. I eventually fired them.

I began wondering what I was going to do. Each time I thought about moving or made the necessary steps to move to another place, God told me, "No, don't get out of place," and "No foreclosure!" I just couldn't understand that because everything pointed to foreclosure. I even contemplated filing bankruptcy, but that wasn't in God's plan either. The money I was going to use to pay the attorney had to be used to pay the gas bill. Of course, I prayed and prayed and prayed and prayed. I wouldn't stop praying. I needed clarity on what I needed to do.

But there's good news! As I was talking to one of my spiritual big sisters Gloria about what I was experiencing, my cell phone rang. It was my mortgage company, and I couldn't believe it. I took the call and explained to my new account representative how I had received the runaround earlier with the loan modification. She told me the best news I'd received in a long time. She said I would be able to apply for the loan modification again. I was so thankful. I did everything she said I needed to do and returned all of my paperwork. I then called to make sure she received it. Such a big load was lifted off my shoulders.

But that didn't last very long. I would apply for a loan modification at least three more times before, in March 2013, I decided to do a short sale of the house, rent a town house, and get my finances in order. Of course, I prayed for direction. This is what God gave me.

On March 19, 2013, the Lord told me: "This move is the beginning of things new for you. The blessings are on the other side. The man you are to meet is on the other side. I can't give you the man now because you are still in the house that is tied to your husband. It only looks bad, but it's not bad… Why are you crying to me? Let's move! I won't let you move to the wrong place. I have your place picked out for you. See my salvation. See my salvation. See my handiwork. I am God, and I know what you need. You need peace. I bring peace. No matter where you live, I am your peace. You will have what you need. I will see to it. Hold on to my Word. I won't steer you wrong. I won't steer you wrong. You will be near people you know. I will send you help. If I helped Jesus bear the cross by sending Simon of Cyrene, I will send you help. I've sent you help all the time. Where I am moving you, you won't have to struggle. You will have more than enough. This part is ending. You have passed through. This is the Red Sea, and the Egyptians you see you will see no more."

Now, look what happened next!

Just before moving in May 2013, my youngest daughter, Mia, was diagnosed with idiopathic adolescent scoliosis. The doctors said the curvature in her spine was over 50 percent and surgery would be necessary. They also said a back brace would not fix the problem. However, her father and I could not bring ourselves to consent to surgery. It was too invasive.

I told the doctors I wanted to wait about two months to find out whether the curvature would progress. Of course, I prayed. Jesus died on the cross for our healing. God made Mia's back. God could (and would) give her a new one. So, I began thanking God for Mia's new spine. In my prayer time, I heard God say that Mia was already healed. I also heard from God that the enemy was going to attempt to make the situation look worse in order to distract me. And that is just what the enemy did. During Mia's appointment in May, the curvature had gotten worse. It was almost 60 percent. I still didn't consent to surgery. I requested that Mia be fitted for a back brace, and the doctors obliged.

Mia was fitted for the back brace, and two weeks later, she received it. When she took an X-ray with the back brace on, there was a substantial improvement in the curve. God continues to tell me that He has already healed Mia, and I believe Him. During my prayer time, God spoke the following to me regarding Mia's diagnosis: "This is the enemy's attempt to make Mia bow. She is covered and will not bow. No fear. She'll be fine."

We moved into our new town-house apartment on May 24, 2013. I had to get used to living in a smaller place. In August 2013, someone broke into the apartment—twice. During both burglaries, the items stolen were my laptop, my daughter's laptop, a Wii console, my bedroom television, my jewelry, and two guns. They even attempted to steal my living room television but couldn't get it out of the house.

I was dumbfounded. How could this be? This was not what God had spoken to me in March. I went back and read again what God said to me about moving. I prayed about the situation and received comfort from the Lord. He said this was a distraction from the enemy and I was to stay focused. So, that is what I did.

These situations reminded me of many biblical accounts, but two come to my mind. One is the story of the three Hebrew boys. They were thrown in a fiery furnace because they would not bow down to an idol statue. What was meant for their demise was turned around for them. They didn't even smell like smoke or have their clothing burned. They didn't look like what they had been through.

The final story is of Peter walking on the water. On a boat ride during a storm, Jesus was witnessed walking on the water. All the disciples watched in bewilderment, except for Peter. He was bold enough to step out of the water and walk as well. Even though he momentarily took his eyes off Jesus and began to sink, he quickly put his gaze back on Jesus and walked on the water again.

These stories describe me. I'm an overcoming water walker. I will not make a decision about my future based on outside circumstances, and neither should you. My situations looked really grim, but each time, God turned things around for me.

Your situation may look grim. You may have even been evicted. You may be receiving chemotherapy treatment for cancer. You may have been fired. Your spouse may have divorced you. Your kids may have turned their backs on you. You may be standing alone in the natural. But focus your gaze on God. He is always with you.

LESSON #5

God Keeps His Promises

God is not a man that he should like; neither the son of
man that he should repent; hath he said, and shall he not do
it? Or hath he spoken, and shall he not make it good?
—Numbers 23:19 NKJV

I was never more afraid in my life. I felt like a deer in headlights. I knew
I had to make decisions about many things, such as the bills, the house,
the children, work, et cetera. But my mind was twirling around like a
tornado. All I could think about was what I had lost. All I kept thinking
was that I had lost my brother, my parents, my husband, and my house.
I had plenty of pity parties—alone, of course. Not many people want to
attend. Yes, misery does love company, but most times, misery is alone.

God spoke many promises to me about my life. The first thing He
told me was He would take care of my bills. When my husband and I
separated and ultimately divorced, I went from a two-income household
to one. However, the expenses were still the same. I was afraid that
utilities would get cut off. I was afraid I wouldn't be able to feed my
girls or buy them clothing.

One Sunday while I was working in the finance department after
church, I heard God tell me, "Because you take care of the bills in my
house, I will take care of the bills in your house." It made me feel very

good to get the reminder that God cares about every aspect of my life. I hadn't forgotten, but I had gotten so caught up in how things looked that I needed a reminder that God sees all and cares.

The second thing He said to me was that I would not go through a foreclosure. When my husband and I first separated, I contemplated moving, but God told me not to get out of my place. I stayed in the house, struggling to pay the house note for almost a year.

When the divorce was finalized, I was awarded the house; however, I had to get it refinanced in my name only. I was not able to do that because my credit was not good enough. I tried to modify the home loan in an effort to improve my credit score. If I was able to have my mortgage lowered, I would be able to improve my credit score.

I applied for a loan modification several times within twelve months and kept being denied. Each time, the mortgage company gave me different reasons. The mortgage company gave me the runaround by having me reapply for a loan modification. While I was applying for these loan modifications, the house note still wasn't being paid and my credit score was getting increasingly worse. This continued for over twelve months.

I was becoming afraid that a foreclosure was imminent. But I kept remembering God's promise: I would not go through a foreclosure. After much prayer, God released me to move from the house. I agreed to do a short sale of the house and rent a town house.

The short-sale process went through smoothly. I was still hurt because I felt like I was losing the house. However, the Lord reminded me that I was not going through a foreclosure. He also reminded me of one of His promises in Malachi 3:11, "And I will rebuke the devourer for your sakes, and he shall not destroy the fruits of your ground; neither shall your vine cast her fruit before the time in the field, saith the Lord of hosts." I was so consumed with having to move from the house that I failed to see that I had stayed in the house for over a year without being evicted by foreclosure and that normally doesn't happen. According to the mortgage company, they were surprised I was in the house that long without a foreclosure.

The third thing He promised was when I let the things of the past go, he would give me more. When I moved, I exhausted myself trying to take everything with me. It didn't matter whether I had the room. My girls would jokingly say I was being a "hoarder" because I kept trying to take so many things to the new place. I remember God telling me to take the things I cherished the most and leave everything else behind; He would give me new things. So, I gave away and threw away a lot of things.

In addition to God's promises specific to me that I mentioned above, I meditated on several of God's promises, such as these mentioned:

- Philippians 4:19, "But my God shall supply all your needs according to his riches in glory by Christ Jesus."
- Psalms 103:1–5, "Praise the LORD, my soul; all my inmost being, praise his holy name. Praise the LORD, my soul, and forget not all his benefits—who forgives all your sins and heals all your diseases, who redeems your life from the pit and crowns you with love and compassion, who satisfies your desires with good things so that your youth is renewed like the eagles."
- ISAIAH 45:2–3, "I will go before you and make the crooked places straight; I will break in pieces the gates of bronze and cut the bars of iron. I will give you the treasures of darkness and hidden riches of secret places, that you may know that I, the LORD, Who call you by your name, I Am the God of Israel."

You can rely on God's Word. His Word gives truth, freedom, life, strength, joy, peace, and love to mention a few things. When you are going through a difficult moment (or moments), mediate on God's Word. It will take work, discipline, and dedication, but the payoff is worth it.

LESSON #6

You're an Overcomer; The Devil Belongs under Your Feet, Not in Your Ear!

And He said to them, "I saw Satan fall like lightning from heaven. Behold, I give you the authority to trample on serpents and scorpions, and over all the power of the enemy, and nothing shall by any means hurt you."
—Luke 10:18–19 NKJV

I always thought I was pretty tough, but as I was going through the onslaught of problems, I was *terrified, confused, and uncertain about my future.* I worried—a lot. How was I going to be able to take care of the kids? How was I going to pay bills? Why was this happening to me? It felt like a whirlwind in my head. I immersed myself in church activities. The girls and I stayed busy. I stayed up late at night so I would be too sleepy to think about what was going on. I received bills on top of bills. I struggled to pay them. I robbed Peter, Paul, Tom, Dick, and Harry to pay bills. For me, it was tough.

I was having trouble concentrating, especially at work. In the midst of my divorce, a new boss began working in my department. During that time, I was behind on bills. I was trying to pay my attorney and just to figure out what was going to happen to me.

In addition to the natural things happening, my self-image and self-confidence were extremely low. I felt stupid, unwanted, and unattractive. There were times at work where simple tasks that I performed all the time, such as remembering suspense dates, were difficult to handle. I would begin working on one thing, and if I was interrupted by a phone call or a visit, I would totally forget what I was doing.

Also, to heap on the pile, my youngest daughter was in the third grade and having difficulties coping with the divorce. It was showing up in her schoolwork. I was getting calls and text messages about something she was or was not doing.

Over time, my new boss began getting angry at me because of my work performance. I don't know, I guess she thought it was deliberate. She was not the type of person I felt I could confide in about what was going on. I confided in her about one particular situation I was having, and she didn't seem to be that concerned.

But God... He constantly talked to me through His Word, in my dreams, and in visitations. God let me know that He had given me the authority to overcome everything I was going through. He let me know that "life and death were in the power of the tongue and those that love it shall eat the fruit thereof." He reminded me through times of prayer that I was to speak to the "dry bones" in my life. I was told that all I had to do was *open my mouth* and tell the enemy to get under *my feet*.

Right after my husband and I separated, I had a dream that was a message of encouragement from God. In the dream, I was chasing this demonic-looking woman with an extremely large tree branch. As I was chasing her, I was hitting her in the head with the tree branch and shouting, "I'm gonna get you!" The woman kept looking back at me with fear as she ran, and I kept hitting her in the head. I talked to one of my spiritual sisters who told me the dream meant I was winning the spiritual warfare with the enemy.

Sometime after the dream, God spoke to me a lot, especially during the night. On April 3, 2013, God spoke the following to me: "I give you abilities to do many things. You can remember. You have clarity. You have gifts that will show through every day. You will be surprised. I give you holy boldness. You will proclaim My name without fear. You will hear Me more and more clearly every day. You will not be able to hear the enemy much because you keep seeking My voice. Abilities, abilities, abilities. I give you abilities to do many things. You will minister to many, sometimes without saying a word. Your walk will minister. People are watching. You have more influence than you think. Oh, the abilities you have. Do them in My name only. I have filled you with so many abilities. They will manifest daily. Those who doubted you will be astonished. Tell them 'to God be the glory.' It will come from Me. All in My timing and I say right now! Receive what I give. Receive the gift of evangelism. That's why you are chaplain of GETEM Worldwide. That's why you work in outreach at church. You will evangelize. You will be alone. You will have very few friends, but those you have will strengthen you. You and your mate will be a mighty force in evangelism. You two will do mighty things in My name. The enemy belongs under your feet and not in your ear. Stomp him down with your words."

Then, on May 2, 2013, God spoke the following to me: "The tide is shifting. Those who suffer now will suffer no more. Oh, I am turning things around for you. Turnaround time is here." Oh, yes, it is. Praise His name! Two days later, I dreamed that I heard a baby crying.

It was (and still is) very comforting when God speaks or visits. These examples were a tremendous help to me. I knew that God cared about the little things. They kept me going. They kept me sane. I am so thankful to God and to the people He placed in my life to help me.

Always remember that *you* are the one with the power (authority) as a believer in Jesus Christ. With your words, you put the enemy (the devil and his cohorts) in their place. As God told me, "The enemy belongs under your feet and not in your ear." If he's in your ear, that means he's too close to you. Get him out of your earshot, and put your feet on his neck!

LESSON #7

You Will Make It to the Other Side

And the same day, when the even was come, he saith
unto them, "Let's pass over unto the other side."
—Mark 4:35 NKJV

There is one story in the Bible that I absolutely love. It was a great
source of encouragement to me during hard times. It is the story found
in Mark 4:35–42.

> On the same day, when evening had come, He said to
> them, "Let us cross over to the other side." Now when
> they had left the multitude, they took Him along in the
> boat as He was. And other little boats were also with
> Him. And a great windstorm arose, and the waves beat
> into the boat, so that it was already filling. But He was
> in the stern, asleep on a pillow. And they awoke Him
> and said to Him, "Teacher, do You not care that we are
> perishing?"
>
> Then He arose and rebuked the wind, and said to the
> sea, "Peace, be still!" And the wind ceased and there
> was a great calm. But He said to them, "Why are you

so fearful? How is it that you have no faith?" And they feared exceedingly, and said to one another, "Who can this be, that even the wind and the sea obey Him?"

In this particular story, Jesus had just finished teaching a multitude of people about the kingdom of God through the use of parables. He and the disciples were leaving the multitude by boat. Just before getting on the boat, Jesus told His disciples, "Let us cross over to the other side." While they were on the boat, a storm arose that rocked the boat. Everyone was panicking, but Jesus was asleep in the lower part of the boat. After the disciples woke Jesus up and questioned Him about whether He cared they were perishing, Jesus rebuked the wind and said to the sea, "Peace, be still." The stormed cleared up instantly, and Jesus rebuked the disciples for being so fearful. The disciples were astonished that the wind and sea obeyed Jesus.

When I studied this particular story, God revealed several things to me regarding my situation. One thing he revealed was that Jesus told the disciples *before* the storm arose, "Let us cross over to the other side." He is saying the same thing to me. God knew these storms were coming before I did, and He knew I would cross over to the other side.

The second thing God revealed to me was that He would be with me. The disciples and Jesus were on the boat during the storm. The difference was that Jesus was not worried. While I was going through my storms, Jesus was right there with me and He was not worried about anything. He knew my bills would be paid. He knew my children and I would eat. He knew my broken heart would be healed. He knew that everything that was lost would be recovered. I was not alone.

The third thing God revealed to me was that I did not have to be fearful because I had the ability to speak to the storms myself. Proverbs 18:20–22 states, "A man's stomach shall be satisfied from the fruit of his mouth; from the produce of his lips, he shall be filled. Death and life are in the power of the tongue, And those who love it will eat its fruit."

The disciples were learning that they had the ability to tell the wind and sea, "Peace, be still," just as Jesus did. Since I am created in the image and likeness of God, I can do the same thing. All I had to do was stop being fearful, open my mouth, and speak to my circumstances. There have been times when, while in my prayer closet, I would hear God tell me in a still, soft voice, "Veronica, speak to your dry bones."

Not only did God lead me to scripture, but God spoke words of encouragement to me during my times of prayer and many times during the night while everyone was asleep. Listed below are just a few of things God said specifically to me:

- June 28, 2013, God said to me: "I am bringing you out of obscurity. I am bringing you to the forefront. Those who thought you were incapable will see My hand in your life. They will see the talents I have placed in you. I will shine the light on you so they will see me. I am pleased that you know I am your source. I am pleased that you are teachable. I will teach you by the Holy Spirit. I will teach you what you need to know. Don't try to figure it out. I will show you each step. Listen for My voice. I will show you how and when. Yes, it's time... I am teaching you, molding you, taking you to where you should go. You're ready for the next step. Go forth. Be ye ready. Boldness is yours now. Go!"
- July 12, 2013, God said to me, "You have many things on your mind, My child. Don't worry. I will give you the help you need."
- July 24, 2013, God said to me, "Walking in the fruit of the spirit helps you make it through problems."
- July 28, 2013, God said to me, "It doesn't matter who doesn't recognize your gifts. I called you. You do what I say. You are Mine!"

- September 2, 2013, God said to me through one of my spiritual sisters, "Your days of being last are over. Promotion is on the way. God is preparing a table before your enemies."
- October 21, 2013, God said to me, "I am healing your heart. I am healing your emotions. I am healing your mind. You are not less than. You are not the tail. You are not last. I already told you that. Be careful not to put negative words in the atmosphere. Promotion time is here. The enemy knows it, and he is trying to talk you out of it. Focus on Me."

The Bible states that God is no respecter of person. If God did these things to encourage me, He will do this to encourage others. Just know that as Jesus told the disciples and me, "Let us cross over to the other side," He is saying the same thing to you also. You will make it to the other side of your negative circumstances just as I did, and Jesus will be right there with you just as He was with me.

LESSON #8

There Is a New Beginning

Behold, I will do a new thing; now it shall spring
forth; shall ye not know it? I will even make a way
in the wilderness and rivers in the desert.
—Isaiah 43:19 NKJV

There is a reason there are eight lessons learned during the journey to my
new beginning. As a matter of fact, in Bible numerology, the number
8 means "new beginnings, regeneration, and victory." The number 8 is
the start of a new thing. Let me explain; the number 7 is the number
of completion, so naturally, the number 8 is the start of something new.

If you look in the Bible, God called for Hebrew baby boys to be
circumcised at eight days old. There were eight survivors of the great
flood during Noah's day with Noah being the eighth person off of the
ark. God made eight covenants with Abraham.

When I analyzed the course of events in my life, I saw there were eight
that were major losses for me. These major losses are:

1. death of my brother in 1992
2. my parents' divorce around 2001 (meant loss of family unity
   for me)
3. Mother's sickness around 2005

4. Father's death in 2009
5. Mother's death in 2010
6. end of marriage in 2010 with divorce being final in 2011
7. loss of house through short sale in 2013
8. early retirement in 2014 (*new beginning*)

My early retirement, the eighth event, is the start of my new beginning. All those things in my life and in my past that were dear to me are all gone. God has a plan for me. God has something new for me. For some reason, I had to go in another direction in God in order to complete what He has for me to do.

I recall soon after my husband and I separated in 2011, I had a strange dream that seemed so real. In the dream, I woke up to use the restroom. I felt pain in my left hand as I turned the light on. When I looked at my left hand, I noticed my pinky and ring fingers had fallen off. I ran to my bed and saw my fingers in the bed. As I was holding my hand crying, my middle and pointer fingers fell off as well. There was no blood, but it was painful. I lay back down in the bed crying, and then I woke up again. My covers were pulled all the way to my face. I tried to figure out whether I was dreaming or whether my fingers had actually fallen off. I pulled my hands from under the covers and gladly saw all of my fingers intact. However, the dream disturbed me. I prayed to get the meaning of my dream, and I spoke to my spiritual sister who interprets dreams. I was told the dream meant that my hands represented the source of how I made a living (not just job wise), and God was changing that. God was telling me then that He was doing a new thing in my life.

God spoke various things to me regarding these losses to prepare me for the start of my new life.

On March 19, 2013, God spoke the following to me regarding the *move from the house* (as mentioned in lesson 4): "This move is the beginning of things new for you. The blessings are on the other side… It only looks like it's bad. It's not… Why are you crying to Me? Let's move forward. I won't let you move to the wrong place. I have your place picked out, and I'll take you to it. See My salvation. See My handiwork. I am God, and I know what you need. You need peace, and I bring peace. No matter where you live, I am your peace. You will have what you need. I will see to it. Hold on to My Word. I won't steer you wrong… Where I am moving you, you won't have to struggle anymore. You will have more than enough. This part is ending. You've passed through. This is the Red Sea part. The Egyptians you see you will not see anymore."

On March 19, 2013, God spoke the following things to me regarding *my daughters*: "Your daughters are your strength. They are helping you more than you think. They see more than you think. They see your tears and hear your cries. They pray for you and want to help you. They love you so much, just like you love them. They rely on you and know you will always be here for them. I made you their mom because I knew you would be a stable force. You would cover them and shield them. You will raise them to know Me."

On March 31, 2013, God spoke the following things to me regarding *my life and my emotional well-being*: "There's so much love in you and around you. The enemy does not want you to know. He wants you to believe no one cares so he can keep you depressed. Don't believe his lies. So many people love you. I love you. I died for you. I was scourged for you. Your girls love you. I am healing your heart. You have so much hurt. Some of it is Satan's lies that you are unworthy. *Lies*! Some of it is you downing yourself. *Stop it!* I give you grace. Your heart is healed already. The enemy lies that your heart is still broken. Take heart. Be of good cheer. Things are better than you think. I come to encourage you. There are good things all around you. There's love all around you… You are important to so many. No one thinks you are dumb. I am dealing with the few who think you are. They aren't even an issue. What I say is important. I say you are worthy."

On March 31, 2013, God spoke the following things to me regarding a *new relationship*: "There is love all around you. Your heart's desire for a mate is all around you. I heard your prayers. I hear all your prayers. The mate I sent won't be based on the flesh. You two will connect by the heart and by the spirit. He will minister to you, and that's how you will be attracted to each other... He will lift you up with My words. No flowers. No candy. No romance like in the movies. Real love. My kind of love. You two will be together forever because you have My kind of love. He won't leave you because I won't let him. He will stick with you even when you act up. Real love. Real love. Real love. Real love. Deep down, you will be secure. He will minister to you deep down. He won't yell. He won't cheat. Real love, I am sending you, and it won't take years, but it will be real soon. Stop fretting. Don't fret. You will desire your mate not physically but emotionally and spiritually. It will be physical but not yet. Marriage. Marriage. Because you take care of My house, I will take care of your house. The new man will raise you up financially too. You two will give big to kingdom work. Be of good cheer. Your man is coming. I am sending him. He's coming soon. Cheer up. Be encouraged. You already have the love you cry for."

On December 3, 2013, God spoke the following things to me regarding my *early retirement*: "Finish the book. This is a time to rest mind and emotions. Another job too soon will still be too stressful. I will let you do little odd jobs but nothing major. Time for your testimony to be brought forth. I will give you peace. I will tell you what to write. I will open the door for the book to be published. I will open the door to employment, but it will not be what you think. Don't tell many what you are doing. A lot of people will not understand. It doesn't matter. Follow My instructions. I take the foolish things of this world to confound the wise. I made a way of escape for you on the job. Rest your emotions. Rest your mind. I will speak, and you will be able to hear Me even more. Heightened discernment. I am raising you up."

Again on December 31, 2013, God spoke the following things to me regarding finding a job after retiring: "Your job will not be what you think your job will be."

I have finally accepted the major losses and changes in my life. I realize that while the enemy sent these things in my life to destroy me, God took them and turned them around for the better. God allowed me to learn many things and showed me that He is to get all of the glory. I have let go of the past. I fully accept the plan God has for me. I am ready for where this journey has taken me. I am grateful that God never left me. Yes, I perceive the new thing God is doing.

I am not the only one who receives a new beginning. You can receive one as well. Each negative circumstance has the potential to make us better people if we allow it. Put your trust in God. Believe His word. A new beginning is yours as well.

My Dreams and Other Spiritual Experiences

But this is what was spoken by the prophet Joel: "And it shall come to pass in the last days, says God, That I will pour out of My Spirit on all flesh; Your sons and your daughters shall prophesy, Your young men shall see visions, Your old men shall dream dreams. And on My menservants and on my maidservants I will pour out My Spirit in those days; And they shall prophesy."
—Acts 2:16–18 NKJV

Being a spirit-filled Christian means that I allow the Holy Spirit to guide my life. During my years of "pressing," the Holy Spirit gave me guidance and encouragement many times. In addition to scripture and various instructions given to me from God Himself, I've had dreams and "spiritual experiences." Some of these experiences may sound crazy to those who do not understand spiritual matters (No, I am not crazy!), but they occurred nonetheless. I've listed a few of them here.

Angelic Visitations

My oldest daughter has seen angels, wings and all (as she puts it), but I haven't. However, I have experienced angelic visitations on a few occasions. I believe these angelic visitations were God's way of letting me know that angels were all around me, protecting me at all times, and that He would never leave me nor forsake me. The visitations were a great comfort to me when I needed it the most.

- While sleeping one night, I heard the sweet voice of a woman talking in my ear. She was speaking some type of language, and I could feel myself responding to her. I then heard the woman tell me, "Wake up." I woke up and felt a calming presence in my room, but I couldn't see anyone. I checked my children's rooms, thinking one of them was trying to wake me up, but they were sound asleep.
- While sleeping one night, I felt someone kick the side of my bed and tell me to wake up and pray. Whoever it was kicked the bed so hard that when I did wake up, the bed was still shaking.
- One night while working on my laptop, I heard footsteps coming down the hallway toward my bedroom. At first, I didn't pay attention because I figured one of my daughters was up. When I looked out into the hallway, I didn't see anyone, but I did see a bright-white sleeve pass by my bedroom. I checked my children's rooms, and they were sound asleep.
- One night while I was up folding laundry, I saw a girl dressed in white standing at the hallway entrance and thought it was my youngest daughter. I instructed her to come get her clothes and put them in her room. When she did not respond, I looked up to repeat my instructions and saw no one in the hallway. I immediately went to my youngest daughter's room. She was asleep.
- While I was at work, I saw several bright, white lights run across the floor unexpectedly. I initially thought it was a mouse because I saw them in my peripheral vision. But I saw the lights again directly.

Dreams

I have had many prophetic dreams. I believe it was God's way of giving me prophetic messages, comfort, and encouragement. I have been having these dreams since 2003. These aren't all of my dreams but a few through which I felt God was trying to convey a message to me.

- I dreamed that a very pretty young lady came to my house and said she wanted to talk to me about the Lord. I invited her into the house, but she did not want to come inside. As she began talking, she stated that Jesus was not the Son of God, He did not die on the cross, and He did not rise from the dead. She also said that Jesus was not the Savior. When she said that, I began quoting scriptures that I didn't realize I knew, proving that Jesus was the Son of God, that He did die on the cross, that He did rise from the dead, and that He is the Savior. As I was talking, the young lady was shaking her head and backing up until she was standing in front of the house across the street. I began screaming at her never to come to my house again, and I called her an anti-Christ. When I woke up from the dream, I was sick to my stomach and had a very bad headache.
- I dreamed that I was watching a husband and wife walk through a house they were wanting to buy. The husband was very arrogant, and the wife was very humble. The husband made comments such as "I can't wait until everyone sees this house," and the wife constantly thanked God for the blessings. As they walked through the house, each room became grander and grander. The first room started off very plain, the next room was a little fancier than the first, and so on. The last room they reached was glorious. It was a sunken living room with a beautiful sectional and crystal chandeliers. When the couple finally left the house and stood on the porch, a voice from the sky said, "Just like the rooms in the house, things may look plain now but they will end luxurious."

- I dreamed that my daughters and I were going to the funeral for one of my ex-husband's uncles. My oldest daughter was about five years old, and my youngest was an infant. When we walked into the church, I noticed that the women sat on one side wearing white and the men sat on the other side wearing black. I also noticed that the deceased was not in a casket but lying on a marble slab and the identity of the deceased kept changing. Each of the men took turns reciting incantations at the body. While they were reciting these incantations, the body would rise from the slab and walk around. But when they stopped, the body would lie back down. This was happening as my daughters and I were being escorted to our seats. When the men finished with their recitations, one of them came to me and said, "Okay, Veronica, it's your turn now."
  I screamed, "*No!*" and woke up.
- I dreamed that my husband and I were in the kitchen preparing dinner. We heard a giant walk across the roof of the house and sit down. We then heard the giant growl, shoot himself, and fall dead on the roof. Suddenly, a hole formed in the ceiling, and blood began streaming through the hole like a waterfall. The blood did not splatter or pool on the floor. It went straight through. I woke up suddenly.
- Sometime in October 2012, I dreamed I was at work sitting at my desk working and a very sweet-sounding voice began speaking to me. I saw nobody, but I could hear the voice audibly. The voice was speaking to me in a language I didn't understand; however, I was speaking the same language back. I was not afraid, and it didn't seem odd for me to hear (or speak to) the voice. When I woke up, I could hear myself still speaking in this same language.
- One day, I fell asleep as I watched Benny Hinn on TV. I dreamed that a creature that looked like one of the flying monkeys from *The Wizard of Oz* (Ha!) suddenly appeared in the TV. The creature walked up to the TV screen, looked at me watching

it, and knocked on the screen. I woke up because I wasn't sure whether I was dreaming or looking at it for real.

Additional Words from God

Throughout this book, I've given you instructions and encouragement that God has given me regarding different circumstances I encountered during my trying times. God speaks to me through the Bible, devotionals, and other people. Sometimes, He speaks to me directly through thoughts. I have heard Him audibly twice in my life.

I have listed information that God has spoken directly to me through thoughts.

- On August 2, 2011, God spoke the following to me through Prophetess/Evangelist Ethel Buchanan: "There's a fear in you that God is snatching away. When you pray, there is a fear that something bad will happen. Take care of God's business. God has given you authority to lose things in the earth realm. You have God's authority from heaven to pull down strongholds even in your house. God sees what you can't see."
- On September 11, 2012, God spoke the following to me: "I love you. You don't have to look to anyone to validate you."
- One night during the spring of 2012, God spoke to me all through the night. I slept, but it wasn't a sound sleep. I could hear God—or rather constant thoughts—cross my mind all night. God told me not to worry about my sins; they were forgiven. He said he would take away sinful desires. He also told me not to worry about my marriage ending. He would send someone who would love me. God told me I was an intercessor, and He was allowing me to get training through GETEM Worldwide so I could work ministry elsewhere. He also told me not to worry about my kids.

- On October 11, 2012, God spoke the following to me by Sister Kimberly Smith: "The Lord says you are dear to Him. He loves you. He is pleased with your life. An imp wants you to think you are invisible."

- On November 24, 2012, God spoke the following to me: "The devil wishes to sift you as wheat. He wants to prove whether your stance for me is real. The attack at work is the devil's way of proving you, and you stood... I am pleased. You've moved up another level."

- On December 2, 2012, God spoke the following to me: "Don't rush your prayer time. Listen for the answer. Push to go deeper. I want you to get answers from me. Don't rely on others for what I say. I will tell you directly, but I will use them too as I will."

- On December 12, 2012, God spoke the following to me: "Rise up, Precious Sister, with healing in your wings. Your body is made new. I give you new blood. I am God, and only I give life. You have work to do. Rise up. You will be My daughter. I am drawing you to Me. Come forth. Healing is yours. Come forth. You have much work. You are a mighty woman of God though you don't see it yourself. You are a mighty strong woman of God. Walk in it *now*! When you rise up, you will have an anointing so powerful you'll know it is God."

- On April 12, 2013, God spoke the following to me: "Pray all the time, not just when you are in trouble, but when things are going well too."

- On May 2, 2013, God spoke the following to me: "Stop the pity party. I will supply you with everything you will need. Don't worry about who won't do what. I will send whom you need to help you when you move. You planted a seed at work when you humbled yourself... You were not prideful. You obeyed My instructions and obedience comes before blessings. More is to come... Promotion is coming. Your move is the forerunner of what's to come. Don't worry about storage. You will have it. Just watch and see it unfold. Greater is He that's within you than He that is in the world. You have Me. I will help you. Don't worry about the outside world. The world takes care of its own. You are not of the world. I will send whom you need. Just watch and see. I will not disappoint. The tide is shifting. Those who suffer now will suffer no more. I'm turning things around for you. Turnaround time is here. Oh, yes, it is! Praise His name!"

- On May 4, 2013, I heard a baby crying while I was asleep. On May 6, 2013, God told me He has given me an overwhelming desire to see souls be saved. I believe that is what the baby crying two days earlier was about.

- On September 29, 2013, God spoke the following to me after my new apartment was burglarized for the second time: "You are on assignment. Pull down strongholds from the complex. But things will get worse before they get better. The land is yours."

- On November 5, 2013, God spoke the following to me regarding work: "You have problems at work with certain people because of who you are in Me. You know who you are outside of work. These people define themselves by their jobs and their credentials. You have what they wish they had. You have My joy and My strength and My peace. They only rely on their jobs. You have much more, and you are really happier than they are."

- On November 18, 2013, God spoke the following to me regarding management at work: "They are acting so mean because you are trampling on Satan's kingdom. Strongholds and demonic chains are being pulled down. Finish the job. Cut the enemy's head off."

- On January 2, 2014, God spoke the following to me: "You will be rewarded as you labor in prayer for others. Your needs will be met. Don't worry. Pull down wickedness in My name. Decree righteousness in My name. Decree healing in My name. Yolks will be destroyed in My name. I give you authority."

- On January 3, 2014, God spoke the following to me regarding my finances after I asked Him to tell me what I was doing wrong regarding my household budget. I had to repent for much: "Check your attitude regarding tithing. It's a direct correlation between your attitude and your financial blessings. Do you tithe out of love or out of fear? I want cheerful givers not fearful givers. I want you to tithe because you love Me not because you are scared of what I will do if you don't tithe… Tithing is not just an act. It's an attitude. Check your attitude. I will help you overcome. I want you to tithe only because you love Me and trust Me. I will take care of you. It's the attitude that counts not just the action. Get past the act. You even give to get. You plant seeds out of fear and selfishness. That's why some things are delayed. Too much fear. Plant seeds out of love and trust, not out of fear. Religion has it all wrong. Tithe and give, but check your heart… You don't really trust Me with your finances. If you did, you would not be so afraid of going under. I told you I would take care of you. You only tithe to keep from being cursed. Your attitude already has you cursed. You decree and declare things as only a religious exercise in hopes of a financial miracle. You don't really believe I will take care of you. Check your heart. The love of money is the root of all evil. You love money even though you don't use it for evil. You feel money is your security. You don't see Me as your source. Check your heart. You want Me to give. You want to be used as a funnel only to make sure your needs are met first. Where is your love for mankind? Check your heart. Be content with what you have. You are interested in gaining stuff. You've fallen for the prosperity teaching. Money is to advance the kingdom. Yes, I bless, but the heart must be right. Your heart isn't right. If I give you too much, you will get corrupted soon after. Check your heart. I will help you. You are lusting after money. Don't lust for money. Go after Me and Me only. Search your heart. Seek to do right. Follow Me. Let the Holy Spirit lead you. That will change your heart. Start praising Me for what you have now. You have food and shelter. Finish the book to help others, not for financial gain."

Finally, God spoke to me in reference to this book. As I mentioned in the beginning, I felt the seed being planted within me when my friend Gloria suggested that I write this book. I knew the idea was from God. I also received prophetic messages through my spiritual sister Kim that this book would be a source of help for many people.

When my apartment was burglarized in August 2013, my laptop was stolen. The manuscript for this book was saved on the laptop; however, I had also saved the manuscript on a thumb drive, which was not stolen. God instructed me to start writing the book again once I replaced the laptop from the insurance settlement I received. Various times after receiving the settlement, I heard God nudging me to complete this book.

- On December 3, 2013, I received the following messages from God in reference to completing this book and early retirement: "Finish the book. This is the time (early retirement) to rest your mind and emotions. Another job too soon will still be too stressful. I will lead you to little odd jobs but nothing major. Time for our testimony to be brought forth. I will give you peace. I will tell you what to write. I will open the door for your book to be published. I will open the door to employment. It will not be what you think. Don't tell many people what you are doing. A lot of people will not understand. It doesn't matter. Follow My instructions. I will take the foolish things of this world to confound the wise. I made a way of escape (from the job)."
- On December 28, 2013, God spoke the following also about the completion of this book: "Finish writing the book. You keep wanting Me to bless you financially, but your blessings are in your obedience to Me in reference to the book. Your only job

right now is to finish the book. I will sustain you. I will take care of you. Stop trying to figure out how. Obey Me, and finish the book. Your breakthrough will come through your obedience to Me."

- On December 31, 2013, God spoke the following again in reference to the completion of this book: "You will finish the book before your retirement. Publishing will be in the works before your retirement. It doesn't take long for Me to do anything."

I pray you were encouraged by reading my testimony. Know that God is always with you, no matter what is going on in your life. Know that God loves you no matter what you have done. Know that God will give you a new beginning just like He did for me.

Dear Lord,

My assignment has been completed. I pray You are pleased with me.

In Jesus's name, amen!